As an experienced marke[...] [...]ding the right words for persuasion. [...] I get a lot more qualified referrals bec[...] [...]cting just the right prospects for the s[...]

Working with Lorraine ha[...] [...]usiness has taken off and I've seen her turn around other entrepreneurs' businesses too!

Harry A. Thomas
Owner, MarketingHat

Lorraine's process and technique was invaluable to launching forward the messaging for our company. We spent too much time telling customers what we weren't rather than what we WERE. Within a day, we were excited to stand behind our new elevator speech and introduce it to our team. It's proven to be a key to our success in the sales process.

Marcie Glenn, CEO
Another Source

In just the few hours I spent with Lorraine, my elevator speech went from average to outstanding. Lorraine is professional and personable, and our work together has instilled a level of confidence in me I never thought possible. Now, with one sentence, I am able to communicate to potential clients what I do and how it will benefit them. This ability to speak clearly is invaluable.

Rachael Eaton
Owner, Time Well Saved

Because my practice is so specialized, I had difficulty explaining to people what I did. I'd spend more time explaining what I *didn't* do! Lorraine's "elevator speech" process helped me identify the unique elements of my approach that were relevant to my ideal clients. From there we came up with a wonderful way to capture people's attention and engage them in conversation about my work.

Wimsey Cherrington
LMP, CTP, aka "The Body Detective"

LORRAINE HOWELL IS a wizard! In the process of developing my elevator speech, I received so much more than I expected. Because I have a developing business, I continue to refine what my business model is and will be. Lorraine's elevator speech methodology actually helped me clarify exactly what I do well AND how to talk about it clearly and succinctly. I walked into the session with anxiety and trepidation and walked out with clarity and confidence. Lorraine helped me put into words what is in my gut. Thank you, Lorraine, for your amazing gift of the elevator speech and all that goes with it.

Jeanne Watanabe
Owner/Broker, 360 Home

WHEN I STARTED a new career path, I was struggling with how to introduce myself and the service I had to offer. Lorraine spent just two hours with me to develop the perfect opening line: "I lead groups of CEOs who help each other to grow their businesses." Instantly I was able to speak with confidence about what I do, which led people to ask more questions, giving me the opportunity to tell people about what I did in a way that made sense for me and was understandable for them. Working with Lorraine completely changed my outlook and my income! Until that point, I was really struggling getting new clients. Now my client base is overflowing and I don't believe it would have been possible had I not worked with Lorraine to develop my elevator speech with both confidence and impact!

Mary (Allan) Marshall
Senior VP-Western Division
Vistage International, Inc.

BEING IN AN industry that offers over 750,000 products with 21,000 competitors, we needed a simple but effective way of communicating our elevator speech. Lorraine was able to unearth a gem after spending a morning with our team. Her ability to thoughtfully understand our company and challenge us to consider what we really do sets her apart from the pack. She even makes the process fun!

Matthew Mason
VP Business Development
PromoShop

GIVE YOUR ELEVATOR SPEECH A LIFT!

SECOND EDITION

LORRAINE HOWELL

Book Publishers Network
P.O. Box 2256
Bothell • WA • 98041
Pн • 425-483-3040

First edition, 2006
   First printing, June 2006
   Second printing, November 2007

Second edition, 2010
   First printing, July 2010

10 9 8 7 6 5 4

Printed in the United States of America

   LCCN 2006926021
   ISBN 10: 1-887542-39-6
   ISBN 13: 978-1-887542-39-5

Editor: Vicki McCown and Julie Scandora
Cover Design: Laura Zugzda
Interior Layout: Stephanie Martindale

DEDICATION

THIS BOOK IS dedicated to my amazing husband, David, and our son, Matthew. Your love, laughter, and support make all things possible!

CONTENTS

PREFACE

SINCE I PUBLISHED the first edition of this book in 2006, the business world has experienced tremendous changes. The U.S. and global economies have seen seismic shifts, and the social media revolution has transformed the marketplace for entrepreneurs and people seeking employment. However, the basics for clear, concise, and memorable communication are more critical today if you want to stand out from the crowd.

Because of the big changes in the employment landscape, more clients began asking for my help with crafting personal elevator speeches they could use for job searches and career transitions. And the concept of creating a personal brand has emerged for people who are either entering the job market for the first time or repositioning themselves for new opportunities.

The new Chapter Eight, Elevator Speeches and Your Personal Branding, details how to adjust the basic elevator speech questionnaire to your personal branding statement. The foundational concepts remain the same; your answers change based on your new audience: prospective employers or referral contacts.

Social media has added a new wrinkle to the mix. The fundamentals are the same ... the medium has changed. Sites like LinkedIn and Facebook have given everyone a worldwide audience.

However, the speed of tweeting, texting, blogging, et al. makes it more imperative to think before you tweet! This is particularly important when you are considering engaging journalists and other new media outlets. Chapter Ten, Helpful Hints for Speaking to the Media, adds new tips in this area.

SECOND EDITION ACKNOWLEDGEMENTS

Thank you to Kathy Berggren, Senior Lecturer, Communication Department, Cornell University, and her students for their valuable feedback. Their comments from their class experience with the book helped crystallize the new elements needed for this edition and suggested more ideas for people new to the job market or making career transitions.

ACKNOWLEDGEMENTS

As THE SAYING goes "It takes a village..." And my village includes so many people who helped me birth this project and deserve my gratitude and recognition.

A big thank you to Dr. Julie Miller (Business Writing That Counts!) who relentlessly held my feet to the fire until this book went to print. She also shared everything she learned about writing and publishing so that I could benefit from her experience. To the rest of our WBO Business Building Group, Peggy Jacobson and Eva Chiu, thank you for providing a safe and supportive sounding board while I developed and grew my business.

I have had the privilege and benefit of working with an amazing group of colleagues led by Mary Allan, of Vistage, formerly TEC International. Thank you to Mary, Andrea, Carol, Clara, David, Harry, Jeanette, Jeanne, Lynne, Mikelann, Rodger, Sheila, Simone, and Susan.

They gave me insight, feedback, and accountability in monthly doses for the past three years.

My membership and involvement in several organizations have provided me the environment to develop, practice, and fine tune my elevator speech process, and have given me opportunities to practice what I preach. Many thanks to my friends and colleagues in Women

Business Owners (WBO), Association of Women in Communications (AWC), Public Relations Society of America (PRSA), Northwest Chapter of the National Speakers Association (NSA), Greater Seattle Chamber of Commerce, and Executive Women International (EWI), the WNET staff at the Seattle office of the U.S. Small Business Administration, and the Columbia Tower Club.

To my wonderful clients, whose many stories are included here, thank you for your trust and your business. It is an honor and a pleasure to work with you.

The title for this book came from a serendipitous collaboration between the talented people at Nancy S. Juetten Marketing, Inc. and Michael Courtney Design, Inc. Thank you for your insight and creativity.

To the team at Book Publishers Network, thank you for guiding me through this adventure. Vicki McCown, editor, gave my words oomph and clarity. Stephanie Martindale added creativity and life to the layout. Laura Zugzda patiently worked out the cover design that was just right. And many thanks to publisher Sheryn Hara, who walked with me step-by-step on this journey. She gave me confidence throughout.

I am blessed with wonderful friends whose love and support I cherish. They also provided useful feedback which I incorporated in the book. Thank you Carol Vipperman, Jeta McKillip, Steve Borstad, and Barbara Setters.

And my family…Thank you! My mother, Katherine, showed me the value of listening to my gut. My brother Stuart, and my sisters Nikki, Linda, and Patti, inspire me. My in-laws Sally F., Sally W., Patti, and Mike surround me with love and unconditional acceptance. Thank you all for your love and support.

INTRODUCTION

YOU HAVE THIRTY seconds or less to capture someone's interest in what you have to say. In this fast-paced, information-overloaded, multimedia society, we are all channel surfing for information that is useful or relevant to us. We all have "remote controls" in our brains. We scan constantly and stop only when we see or hear something that interests us. We do it with television, we do it on the Internet, and we do it in conversation. That's why the elevator speech has become an essential communication tool.

An elevator speech is a short, pithy sentence or two that tells people, in a nutshell, what you do for a living. The catchy title "elevator speech" refers to the amount of time you have to generate interest with another person. For example, if you get on at the top floor of a forty-story building and ride down in an elevator nonstop to the lobby, it takes about twenty seconds. In that amount of time, you should be able to explain to another person—or a room full of people—what you do or what your business does. And if you do it well, what you say will engage your audience and prompt them to ask more questions.

Soon after I started teaching media interview skills, I realized my clients felt intimidated, either because they were unsure about the main points they wanted to communicate or were unfocused in their delivery. I created an easy practical process that enabled people to focus on the listeners, identify the desired outcome of the communication, and create clear and concise phrasing that connects with the intended audience.

As I branched out into public speaking and presentation coaching, my clients asked for my help in creating engaging ways to talk about themselves and their businesses at networking events or when they encountered marketing opportunities. So, I have adapted this effective process, creating a tool dozens of business owners have used to produce memorable "elevator speeches." The results have been amazingly successful, as you will see in the upcoming examples.

People in business have the opportunity to talk about what they do several times each week. The most frequently asked question when two people meet is "What do you do?" Whether you're attending networking events, business meetings, or social occasions, having an engaging way to answer that question can make the difference in whether or not you develop a future relationship with a client or a generate a new source for referrals.

This book is designed to help you create a memorable elevator speech. By the end of the book, you will also have a quick and easy step-by-step process you can use anytime you are called upon to give a speech, presentation, or media interview.

There are a few things to remember as you read through and use the steps in this book. First, your elevator speech is not supposed to tell people everything all at once. It is a conversation starter. There's nothing that stops a conversation dead in its tracks more quickly and more often than information overload. The idea is to make your initial statements concise and intriguing. Think of it as a teaser or a movie trailer. A great elevator speech arouses your listeners' interest and compels them to ask for more information.

Second, an elevator speech is not a canned spiel you rattle off anytime someone asks you what you do. Nor is it set in stone. An elevator speech is a living tool that you fine-tune and adjust depending on your audience and the situation. So, when you create an elevator speech, pay attention to how it is received and the reaction it generates. That will tell you what changes are needed and when.

And finally, there is no one formula for creating a perfect elevator speech. However, utilizing the answers to the questions detailed in this book, preferably in the order in which they are presented, will lead you to your elevator speech—sometimes in very surprising ways.

This process works for both individuals and groups. To craft your personal elevator speech, you can choose to go through the questions on your own or invite a few friends or colleagues to help you. To create an elevator speech for a company, employees can work through this process as a team and come up with language that everyone can use to talk about the organization.

Chapters One through Six are based on the questionnaire, shown on page xvi, and explain the thinking behind the questions. Answering the questionnaire is the first step in the process I developed. Chapter Seven explains the second step: how to put all the pieces together into an elevator speech. Chapter Eight highlights the concept of "personal branding" and how your elevator speech is an important tool in building your personal brand and landing a job or navigating a career change. Chapters Nine and Ten show how to use this process for speeches, presentations, and media interviews, including new Web and social media. Chapter Eleven offers tips and strategies for keeping your elevator speech, your personal thirty-second commercial, fresh and relevant.

How to Use This Book

THIS BOOK IS the written version of a popular workshop I developed to help entrepreneurs, business people, and other professionals describe what they do in a clear, concise, engaging way. The format follows the basic questionnaire I use in my trainings and seminars—questions that will enable you to focus on the essential elements every communication needs to engage a listener's interest in what you have to say.

We will focus first on your audience: who they are, what interests they have, and reasons why they would be interested in your message. Once you have answered those questions and explored those answers in depth, key ideas will emerge. Then you will be ready to put them all together in a series of phrases and sentences that will connect with your enthusiasm and spark interest from your listener.

This process works not only for developing an elevator speech, but also in creating content for speeches and presentations. And it provides you with a critical tool if you ever decide to talk to anyone in the media. Later chapters show you how to adjust slightly the questions and use the answers from those questions to create key phrases and ideas for other forms of public communication. At the end of each chapter, "In a Nutshell…" highlights the main points to remember.

The questionnaire below is designed to elicit key concepts, words, and phrases that can be used to craft your elevator speech. These questions also form the foundation for other verbal communications including speeches, presentations, and media interviews.

ELEVATOR SPEECH QUESTIONNAIRE

1. Who is your target audience?
2. What do they care about?
3. Why should they do business with you? WIIFT?
4. What do you do? What results do you provide?
5. What are you selling? (How do you want people to feel when they work with you?)
6. What spins your jets about your business?
7. What do you do better than anyone else? (What is your specialty?)
8. What would your best clients/customers say about you?
9. Can you give an example of one successful project?
10. What do you want people to remember about you and your service?

Ground Floor

The First Question

Heal th care
Law yers
Business

Business + Team Leaders/reps
Execs, Lawyers, personal
Speaking

THIS CHAPTER COVERS Question #1: "Who is your target audience?" Another way to ask the same question is "Who is your target market?" It is essential to know who you are trying to reach or influence.

This may seem like an elementary question, especially for someone in business. But to really make the connection with your intended audience(s), you need to answer the question in depth. Identifying your target audience/market also enables you to qualify your leads and prospects.

This first area of questioning often creates obstacles, especially for new entrepreneurs. Because they view everyone as a potential customer, they are reluctant to define a targeted audience or customer too narrowly. They fear they will lose business by not appealing to more people.

In fact, the opposite is true. When you define your target market, a higher percentage of the people you talk to will recognize what you do and the value you offer. They will automatically be interested in what you do because they need it. They will beat a path to your door and bring others with them who can find uses for what you offer.

1

For example, I began working with an accomplished litigation attorney who left the courtroom wars and decided to develop a business to "help the little guys," as she put it. Her goal was to teach negotiating skills and offer negotiating consultations to business owners.

In answer to the question "What do you do?" she would reply, "I teach negotiation skills to businesses." Then what followed was usually a detailed explanation about why people needed her services and how she worked.

In addition to networking, she would do public speaking to market herself. A fabulous speaker, she connected well with her audiences and demonstrated a depth of knowledge about her topic. Yet people were slow to hire her or recommend her to others.

Clearly her marketing strategy was not working; either the people she spoke to did not represent her ideal customers or she wasn't communicating well what she had to offer. It's possible that when people heard that she could teach them how to negotiate, they may have interpreted it to mean she taught the art of compromise. And who wants to compromise in business??? We all want to win!

So we went to work on crafting a new way for her to talk about her services. When I first asked, "Who is your target audience or your ideal customer?" she answered "Small to mid-size companies in the $3 million to $50 million range."

I asked more questions and we dug a little deeper. What was going on with these companies? What specific activities did they have in common? Why would they need her services? What problems were they having? Once we uncovered the characteristics of her ideal customers, we were able to define her target market more narrowly: small to mid-size companies that acted as vendors to large multinational corporations.

The principal characteristics of her target market were not defined by their gross sales or income, but rather by their activities. For these companies to be successful, they needed to know how to negotiate contracts and agreements successfully with larger international entities.

Once we narrowed the field of opportunity, it became much easier to develop a focused message those small to mid-size companies would recognize. It also became easier for referral sources to recognize who might be potential clients.

Almost immediately, my client moved from explaining the complexities of negotiating to stating the problems she could solve for any company that had vendor relationships with large, multinational corporations. (We'll discuss those specifics in a later chapter!) Her phone started ringing and it hasn't stopped since!

Another client had trouble explaining what his new consulting business offered potential clients. Even though people could see he had good skills and information, no one seemed to understand exactly what he did. When asked about his business, he would say that he was a consultant who helps businesses run better.

This client had worked previously as a project manager for a large aerospace manufacturing company. He had been responsible for successfully bringing several new products from the idea phase to market. After weathering several layoffs and consolidations, he decided to take his expertise into the marketplace and work with new companies to develop great ideas.

But he had made the common mistake of marketing to any and every business owner he talked to, thinking that he didn't want to pass up any possible opportunity. Unfortunately, his message was so broad that no one recognized what he could do for them or anyone else.

After delving into the specifics of his target audience, we discovered he could be most helpful to entrepreneurs who were in the start-up stage. His specialty and passion were taking a company from the idea phase to a viable and working business. And that formed the foundation of his elevator speech. His opening line changed to "a consultant who helps entrepreneurs turn great ideas into great businesses."

Once we discovered who his ideal customer would be, we could then move on to the rest of the questions, with each answer bringing us closer to a clear and concise elevator speech.

Another example of what answering the "Who is your target audience?" question can do for you comes from a client who is a very creative organizer. She works with people who need to turn chaos into order in the office or home. She will also do errands and projects that can be delegated to a third party.

Similar to the project manager, she had been marketing to just about everybody, because, after all, who doesn't need a little more organization in their lives? But the fact was she loved working for busy executives and stay-at-home moms and dads, two completely different but specific markets. Once we identified those two separate groups of customers, we were able to focus on the needs of each one and create messages that would be recognized by each type of customer. Developing those messages begins in Chapter Two when we start looking at the needs of your target customers

A final example of identifying your target market illustrates how doing so can qualify your leads and prospects. When you are specific, people will self-select, so you don't have to waste time marketing to people who would never hire you.

One of my colleagues discovered this additional benefit when we crafted his new elevator speech. He is a marketing expert, promoting his ability to stimulate innovation via workshops and seminars. He thought if he could demonstrate his brilliant ability to ask the right marketing questions and how that leads to innovation, people would hire him to coach and train marketing teams.

But something was missing in the message. While people enjoyed his workshops and public speaking, he wasn't generating much follow-up business.

We went to work on his elevator speech and discovered that he really wanted to be a "marketing director for hire." His target market/audience was companies that knew they needed marketing help, but didn't know exactly what kind of help that would be. And that became his elevator speech! When asked what he does, he will tell you "I'm a marketing director for hire for companies that need marketing help but are not sure where to start."

We crafted a speech to reflect this shift in his focus and how he talked about his business. The response he received in the marketplace changed immediately. People who were in a marketing muddle recognized how he could help them. And he no longer got trapped into dead-end conversations with people who didn't need what he had to offer. The results? He has more qualified leads and prospects, an increase in new business, and a great deal of personal excitement about his future as an entrepreneur.

Up to this point, the stories I've related have involved individual business owners and service providers. However, companies and large corporations must also identify and clearly define their audiences. But, more often than not, the elevator speech for a company is shaped by the interests and concerns of their target market, rather than their characteristics. And that leads us to Question #2 in crafting a great elevator speech.

In a Nutshell...

1) Being clear about who you are trying to reach is the first step in crafting an effective "elevator speech."

2) Identify your target audience, a.k.a. your ideal customers or clients.

3) Look a little deeper. What specific characteristics emerge?

   Helpful questions to ask:
   a. What activities do they have in common?
   b. Is their industry expanding or contracting?
   c. What problems or issues do they have?
   d. Why would they need your product or service?

Second Floor

What Do They Care About?

Question #2 on the Elevator Speech questionnaire is: What does your target audience or customer care about? Other ways to ask this are: What is important to them? What are the issues or problems they face in day-to-day business?

When you look at what your audience cares about, put yourself in their shoes. The question is not "What do YOU think they should care about?" Rather, you want to ask "From their perspective, what is important to them?"

Often we are so intent on what we have to say, we completely forget to consider what is on the mind of the listener. In a typical networking situation, we are rushing to tell people as much as we can about the features and benefits of our product or service. We are not thinking about what may be of interest to the other person. An effective elevator speech will zero in on the concerns or problems facing your target audience.

For business-to-business companies, your target audience usually cares about profits, quality, dependability, service, and speed, plus issues pertaining to their industry. But it is important to look beyond the general categories and get as specific and as detailed as possible. Spend time exploring what customers care about, or what is important to them, because the answers to those questions often become the very language you will use in the elevator speech.

For example, a very successful company had been providing unique employment recruiting services for over fifteen years, yet the owners still found it difficult to explain to people what they did. Most of the time, they told people what they didn't do. They were not an employment agency and they were not headhunters. However, they had been able to build the business because, once recruiters hired them, the value of the service was immediately apparent, insuring long-term relationships.

These people came to me almost as a last resort. They wanted to launch a successful marketing campaign, but they were stuck way back at the elevator speech stage—how to quickly and concisely articulate their service.

The first step of identifying their audience was easy, because they already knew their target market: company recruiters. Next we started looking at what recruiters cared about and identified three key areas: Recruiters want to reduce the risk, the time, and the costs associated with hiring new employees. My client's company had an effective and innovative tool that accomplished all three with remarkable results.

By seeing the connection between their target market and the specific concerns of those potential customers, the framework of their new elevator speech began to emerge. The rest of the pieces came together easily and clearly to create a grabber of a beginning: "We have a revolutionary process for recruiters that reduces the time, costs, and risks involved with hiring new employees." This opening line captures interest about the revolutionary process and tells the listener who needs this service what it does. Now everyone at the company knows how to explain what they do to anyone who asks, especially company recruiters!

Returning to our negotiating expert, we know her ideal clients care about building fair and profitable vendor agreements with large companies. Their economic future depends on being able to live with the current and future conditions written into any contract.

There are many huge companies that have the reputation for riding roughshod over vendors once they have signed on the dotted line. In the beginning, the vendor feels lucky to have such a big distributor of his or her products. Then, year after year, profit margins get squeezed until the vendor can't afford to do business with the company anymore. If the vendor doesn't do it their way, the big guys just move on to someone else. The vendor feels powerless in the process.

That's exactly where our negotiating expert comes in. She understands that small to mid-size vendors want to walk away from the negotiating table feeling as if they have an agreement they can not only live with, but will enable their business to thrive. They don't want to be constantly worried that each year could be their last.

The excitement of getting a huge contract with multinational corporations can come to a screeching halt when it comes time to sit down at the negotiating table facing a high-priced, more experienced legal team. The small vendor wants and needs a level playing field.

And there is my client's elevator speech. "I level the playing field for small to mid-size companies that negotiate vendor contracts with large, multinational corporations." In one sentence she can say exactly what she does, the problem she solves, and who can benefit from her expertise.

Within just a few weeks of creating her new elevator speech, my client was booked solid for seminars, training, and well-paid consulting projects, because people immediately recognized what she did, the value of it, and who would need her negotiating expertise.

And the most surprising development is that some of the multinational companies are recognizing that a level playing field for contract negotiations is improving their vendor relationships. She creates a win-win situation all around, which has opened a whole new market for her services.

Our organizing expert provides another example of understanding the specific needs of your target market. She has two separate and distinct types of clients: busy executives and stay-at-home parents. Each group benefits from the services of a professional organizer, but each group also defines those needs differently. As a result, she adjusts her elevator speech for each audience.

When she's networking at business events, my client tells people she "takes things off their 'to do' list." And when she is talking to busy moms and dads, she explains how she runs errands and organizes cluttered spaces at home. Each message resonates with the group to which it is delivered because it addresses issues specific to them. While the organizing expert is providing similar services for both audiences, each group responds to different marketing approaches.

If you are unsure about the needs and concerns of your potential customers, then a little market research is required. You can accomplish this simply by doing some informal surveys, either in-person or over the phone. There are also several free Web-based survey tools available. Or, if you have the time and resources, hire a market research company. Knowing as much as you can about your target market is critical to the success of any business. And it is critical to the success of your elevator speech!

In review, we've answered the first two key questions, "Who is your target audience/market/ideal customer?" and "What do they care about?" In the next chapter we start looking at your message and how it relates to these first two questions by asking "What value/results/benefits do you provide?"

In a Nutshell...

1) What is important to your target customers or clients? What issues or problems do they face? (Hint: It's NOT what YOU think they should care about!)

2) If you can't answer the question above, then do a little market research and ask.

3) Do you have what they need?

Third Floor

What Do You Do?

After looking at your audience and what they care about, the next step is to define what you do. This is usually the step that causes so much angst at networking events. People are always telling me "It's so difficult to explain exactly what I *do*!"—especially if it's something like a high-tech business, a bio-tech company, or some other business with complex products and processes. But I have challenged many people to allow me a few minutes to come up with a way to describe what they do that is clear, concise, and generates interest. And I can do so because I understand the real question that needs to be answered.

When people ask "What do you do?" they are really asking, "What can you do for me?" or "What value/benefits/results do you provide?" Another way to think about it is "What is different in the lives of your customers as a result of your product or service?" In other words, what has changed for the better for them as a result of doing business with you? Salespeople will recognize it as a variation of the WIIFT question, shorthand for "What's in it for them?"

Because I have to walk my talk, I continue to work on my own elevator speech, and it changes continuously depending on the person I'm talking to and what area of expertise I want to highlight or market. One of my most effective elevator speeches

11

evolved from the idea that most business executives and community leaders want to make a difference. They want audiences to listen to them and feel empowered or moved to take action. So in addition to telling people that I do media and presentation skills training, I add, "I teach leaders to speak with confidence and impact."

Nearly every time I say that phrase, people will ask me more about what I do, or talk about how they could use that kind of training, or mention they know someone who may need that service. And then they ask for my business card.

Define the results, not the process. To paraphrase an idea I have borrowed from David McCaffrey at Starbucks Coffee Company: "If I ask you what time it is, don't tell me how the watch works!"

I worked with a fast-growing company that provides promotional merchandise companies use as giveaways and incentives. They have a great reputation in the industry and have high-profile Fortune 100 companies as clients. But they wanted to elevate their status in the relationship they had with their customers, moving from simply being the vendor to acting as a partner in the creative process. Instead of being the last call companies made when purchasing promotional merchandise, my clients wanted to be called first so they could be at the table when strategy and outcomes were being discussed. They knew they could provide better service, more competitive prices, and a truly creative, on-target product if they could be part of the initial planning process when companies considered using promotional merchandise.

In this example, it's not the business itself that stands out; it's the way this company does business that makes a difference. And they needed to change their potential customers' perception of them as simply merchandise vendors to valuable partners in the process of selecting and developing promotional merchandise.

We looked at what they actually do for customers, which is to raise the visibility and name recognition of successful businesses as well as extend their brands. Once we defined this, a new elevator speech was born: "We provide promotional merchandise expertise for successful companies that want increased name awareness and brand recognition." In a subsequent media interview, this new elevator speech was quoted verbatim. Another quote used was "We want to become a partner, not just a vendor, in promotional merchandise." Bull's-eye!

Explaining what you do can be challenging for people in certain industries or crowded business sectors. Insurance brokers, financial planners, CPAs, and other professionals in the financial services sector face unique problems when it comes to networking. Often even the people in these professions consider discussing their service—while necessary and beneficial—to be boring, and there's really nothing interesting to say about it. But when you engage someone who is successful in the financial services industry and ask them about their work, it's easy to uncover what differentiates them in the marketplace: They always see the difference they make in their customers' lives by connecting benefits and/or desired results to whatever products or services they provide.

For example, one life insurance salesperson I worked with changed her approach by saying she helped people protect their assets and build wealth. A financial planner changed her elevator speech by saying she's an "expert who helps people who want to retire comfortably and make sure they don't outlive their money." These are two good examples of elevator speeches that are built around the results or benefits provided, not the process or the product. And that's what makes a good elevator speech.

Personal service providers face similar obstacles. I helped a massage therapist come up with a new and imaginative way to talk about her services and she's been using it for several years with great success. Rather than providing the more typical relaxation massage, she specializes in treating people with chronic pain due to illness or injury. She spent most of her time trying to explain the more complex therapies she employed to screen out people who might be looking for traditional massage.

She already had a saying she used, one that explained how she worked with people in chronic pain. As the saying went, "I find, fix it, and send them on their way." But it is the finding and fixing it that differentiates her from other massage therapists. I mentioned that I thought she acted like an investigator, someone looking for clues to find the source of the pain.

Suddenly, the perfect title for her popped into my head. "You're a body detective!"

And that became her opening response when people ask her what she does.

So sometimes it helps to find an alternative way to tell people what you do. If what you do is complicated, look for analogies or metaphors so that in an instant people will understand, be intrigued, and ask you for more details. After all, that's the purpose of the elevator speech…to get your listener to ask you more about what you do.

The "body detective" gets asked about her work every time!

Another client started referring to herself as a specialist in workplace conflict and she explains that it's a lot like "bathing cats." That's an indelible image that captures attention and interest

You can also build an elevator speech around the characteristics of the people you want as clients. For example, maybe you are an expert working with people who are near retirement and they are not sure what decisions they need to make regarding insurance or 401K distributions.

Consider your message from your audience's point of view. What would be of interest or value to them? What do they need? What is the problem you are solving? Why should they care? A good communicator knows how to make the targeted audience care—or at least be more interested.

Within the context of the results you provide, also get specific about your specialty. What do you do better than anyone else? What differentiates you in the marketplace? Is it your market niche, your quality, your service?

Sometimes the connecting ideas are more illusive and intangible. People know they have a need, but may not be able to articulate what the need is. That's why the next question to answer is "What are you selling?"

In a Nutshell...

1) What value/benefits/results do you provide? WIIFT? (What's in it for THEM?)

2) Don't talk about the process; focus on the results. If I ask you what time it is, don't tell me how the watch works!

3) Use examples, analogies, or metaphors to create verbal pictures for your listeners, like the "body detective" and "bathing cats."

Fourth Floor

What Are You Selling?

When I started my business, one of the first places I went to for help was the local office of the U.S. Small Business Administration (SBA). Over the years I have become a big fan of this agency. It's one of the few places where ordinary citizens can get a very direct return on their tax dollars!

I took advantage of the S.C.O.R.E. program, a partner with the SBA. They have volunteers who act as resources and counselors for entrepreneurs. I was fortunate to work with Rich Snow, who at the time was also a professor of marketing at the University of Washington Business School. I had only one appointment with him, but it provided me insight I still use today and pass along to my clients, seminar participants, and now to you.

He asked me one simple question.

"What are you selling?"

I didn't understand him at first. After an initial blank look, I answered, "I'm selling me, my expertise, and experience."

He asked again, "What are you selling?"

I sat, silently wracking my brain for the right answer. Clearly I wasn't getting it!

Finally he explained.

17

"You want to look at what you're selling in the same way marketers of automobiles do. They are not selling the machinery as much as the feeling you get when you sit behind the wheel and turn on the ignition. Automakers are selling power, luxury, status, sex appeal, image, the fountain of youth, safety, family togetherness, etc. They are selling the intangibles, the feelings we want or hope for when we buy that new car."

So when you look at your business, what are YOU selling? What emotions are you tapping into with your product or service? I'm selling confidence, hope, trust, self-esteem, pride, stardom, and the possibility of making a difference. I'm selling all of the intangibles that people hope for when they work on their communication skills, whether is it for speeches, presentations, or media interviews.

But here's an important point. What you are selling is in the mind of your target customer, and that can vary. The negotiating expert is selling fairness to some and a competitive edge to others. All of her customers want a similar outcome, but they often have different views on what is needed to reach those outcomes.

The marketing director for hire is selling convenience, creativity, and solutions to immediate problems. The home health care provider is selling service, compassion, peace of mind, safety, trust.

All of these qualities or intangibles become part of the message. They can be woven into any part of the conversation. But they often work best at the end of the elevator speech, as a wrap-up statement. The negotiating expert might add to her pitch "If you are looking for a competitive edge when you are negotiating with large companies, I can help you gain that edge." The financial planner could say, "If you want to make sure your retirement dreams become a reality, that's my specialty!" And the expert with the innovative recruiting tool could say, "We help you find the right employee fast!" Make your elevator speech appeal to the head and the heart.

In a Nutshell...

1) What are the intangibles associated with your business? What do you want people to think or feel when they buy your product or service?

2) These intangibles can be powerful and persuasive elements in your "elevator speech."

Fifth Floor

What Spins Your Jets?

The next ingredient in your elevator speech can be considered your "secret sauce!" It's your passion, your enthusiasm, and your commitment to the work you do or the cause you are promoting.

When you answer the question "What spins your jets about what you do?" look beyond the obvious or vague answers like "I want to help people" or "I'm very good at what I do." Dig a little deeper.

There are moments in our work when we experience the thrill of making a difference in the lives of others. We solve a particularly thorny problem, or go the extra mile to provide additional service not covered in a contract, or add new insight to a strategic discussion. The experience and the outcome makes all the hard work worthwhile. It's that unmistakable satisfaction that comes from knowing someone else has benefited from your expertise.

If it's been a while since you have considered what turns you on about your work, give it some thought. We often get so busy and stressed, we forget why we chose the work we do. Look at the factors that led you in this direction. Are those factors still relevant and satisfying today?

There are several reasons to look at what lights your fire about your work or your subject matter. The first reason is that communication is about relationships. And people respond positively to another person's passion and enthusiasm. When you become authentic to your listeners, it is much easier to connect with people and move them to take action.

I'm not suggesting that you become all sappy, sugary, hyper, or overambitious about your work. I'm talking about having and communicating a genuine commitment to what you are doing—what gets you up in the morning and keeps you going long after the clock says the work day is over. If you love what you are doing and believe in it, that passion comes through in every way you communicate about it. (And if you don't love what you are doing, then it may be time to make a change. But that's another subject entirely!)

For me, it's that moment when I see my clients suddenly realize that they have overcome their fears about speaking in public or talking to the media. It's that confidence they exude when they finally discover a way to communicate their key messages in a clear, concise, and engaging way. It's the smile on their faces when we pull together the pieces of a difficult puzzle they have been trying to solve for a long time.

The negotiator loves it when her clients feel as if they walked away from the negotiating table with something of value. The financial planner is inspired when the retirement plan she designed for her clients enables them to live their life-long dreams. The promotional merchandise executives are thrilled when they see a T-shirt they created for a client on a tourist at the Great Wall of China!

If you are not sure what sparks your passion, think back to the last time you had a great day at work, or a moment with a customer when you provided just the right solution to a difficult problem. At some point, the thought crossed your mind that went something like "Yeah! That's why I do this work." That is precisely what we are looking for here—that "Aha!" moment for you and your client.

In addition to your communicating authentically, knowing what spins your jets is important because you want people to see themselves as potential customers. If they can see themselves benefiting from working with you or buying your product, then they will self-select. You don't have to "sell" them. They are already sold because of your confidence and certainty that what you are offering is of value.

And passion is powerful—it acts like a magnet. Others see your passion and are drawn to you. And they will tell others about you. You become memorable and you stand out from the crowd. So spend some time identifying what turns you on about your business and don't be afraid to show it appropriately.

In a Nutshell...

1) Your passion, enthusiasm, and commitment produce the "secret sauce" in your "elevator speech."

2) Rediscover what spins your jets (what you love) about what you are doing and use it to begin building authentic relationships with potential customers and referral sources.

Sixth Floor

Other Questions to Ask Yourself

In addition to the first five areas we have explored, there are a few miscellaneous questions that, when answered, often provide some finishing touches to your elevator speech. Asking yourself these questions will help you add depth or clarity when you want to tailor your speech to fit your audience. You'll also come up with some creative ideas to talk about when your listener or audience asks you to explain more about what you do.

The first of these additional questions is "What do your best customers/clients say about you, your product, or your service?" If you don't know the answer to this question or it's been a few years since you asked it, this is a great way to refresh your marketing strategy.

The purpose of this question is to find out what you are doing right. Why are people doing business with you? What are they buying and why? The answer might surprise you. Often people focus on marketing one aspect of their business, yet their customers respond more strongly to something different. And it's possible that you are so close to your own business that you may not recognize what resonates with your customers.

For example, when I first started my business, I talked about the importance of learning the necessary skills for talking to the media and my insider expertise in this area gained from years of working in the industry. But in talking to some of my best clients, I discovered where they found the real value in working with me. Words like "down-to-earth," "comfortable," "safe," "approachable," and "direct" kept popping up in their responses. I soon realized that my skills were appreciated, but it was my ability to be direct in a safe and constructive way that created the strong loyalty that brought repeat business and referrals. I made something my clients found very intimidating much easier, which gave them confidence.

So I started using the language my best clients used when they described my service, because I wanted to work with more people like them. And my "selling" became more like a conversation. I just talked about what I did and used words that describe people's experience in working with me. The rest of the sales process was easy.

Also, if you sometimes feel that selling yourself might be perceived as bragging, using your clients' description of your service can make you feel more confident and at ease. You can say "Our customers tell us…" or "Many of our clients feel…" When you use your own clients' words, what they say becomes a testimonial that highlights key benefits. To paraphrase a familiar "Yellow Pages" tagline: Let your clients do the talking!

Another way to ask this question is "What do you want your reputation to be?" Think of the end-result of your work with people. What do you want them to be saying about you? This is related to the answer to the question of Chapter Five—"What Spins Your Jets?"—because your reputation often deals with the intangibles of relationships.

One client in the home health care and assistance industry wanted a memorable tagline and a new way to talk about his business. Home health care for adults who are disabled due to accidents, chronic disease, or aging is an industry that is exploding in growth. And most companies use words like "trust," "compassion," and "peace of mind" to describe what they offer.

We started looking at what his customers were saying about his services and found the words "kind" and "kindness" kept popping up. And when we talked to his long-term employees and managers about how they saw the company, they continually mentioned the commitment they had to their clients.

We blended those two ideas to create a very powerful statement out of which came a new tagline that could be used for their printed marketing pieces and woven into their elevator speech. Many companies can deliver in-home care and assistance to people in need. But this company delivers that care with "uncompromising commitment and kindness!" Who doesn't want that for their loved ones or family?

So ask your best customers and clients about their experience in working with you. You may even want to hire a market research company to do this. Customers will often be more forthcoming with a third party. What you want is genuine response and feedback, not an automatic and self-conscious compliment.

Next, it's time to develop the success stories you have that demonstrate what you do and the results you provide. What examples do you have of successful projects or interactions with clients? What short scenario can you include in the conversation that shows how you performed and the benefits your customer enjoyed?

I have some short examples I include in my elevator speech. One is the CEO I worked with who went from a C+ to an A- in the evaluations she received of her annual speech to employees. Another is the highly regarded administrator who came to me because she didn't interview well. She landed the job of her dreams after just two coaching sessions. My third example is about the sales team that generated the highest company revenue in years after working with me on their presentation style and content.

In the parlance of career counselors, consider these three points: What was the problem? What action did you take? What were the results? A quick, concise story will show your listener you know what you are doing.

Finally, what do you want people to remember about you? When you have finished the conversation, the phone call, or the sales call, what impression do you want to leave in the minds of your audience? You may want them to be thinking something like "I really like her approach" or "I learned something" or "He really gave us something to think about." Give your listener something worth remembering. When you provide unexpected value in a conversation, you become memorable. And being memorable, in a positive way, is always the objective with a good elevator speech.

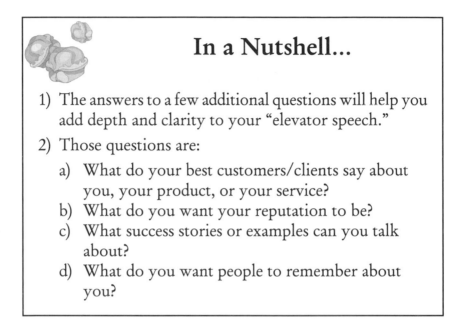

In a Nutshell...

1) The answers to a few additional questions will help you add depth and clarity to your "elevator speech."

2) Those questions are:

   a) What do your best customers/clients say about you, your product, or your service?

   b) What do you want your reputation to be?

   c) What success stories or examples can you talk about?

   d) What do you want people to remember about you?

Seventh Floor

Putting It All Together

As we have seen, once you start asking the right questions, your elevator speech can just jump right out at you. When you shift your focus from what you want to say to the interests and concerns of your target audience, new words and phrases emerge, which you can mix and match depending on your audience and what you want to communicate. You can also shorten your elevator speech to accommodate the circumstances.

For example, for a quick introduction, our negotiating expert simply says, "I help companies level the playing field when they are negotiating with large multi-nationals." At certain networking events, that's all she needs to say for listeners to understand what she does. The executive from the promotional merchandise company could say, "We provide expertise to companies considering the use of promotional merchandise in their marketing."

Your elevator speech is a living, breathing statement you can adjust moment by moment, expanding or contracting the message depending on the audience and the situation. However, whatever you say must sound authentic and natural. You want to be comfortable with and pleased about what you have to say, and the speech must make sense. Create something that *sounds* right when you say it. The words must be words you would use and be easily understood by your audience. This does not mean that you talk down to people. A great elevator speech conveys the message easily, clearly, and quickly.

The next step is to try out your speech and see how people respond. Pay attention to the look on people's faces and what they say back to you when you tell them what you do. If they just look at you and say, "That's nice," and move on, you know your elevator speech needs more work. If they start asking you questions like "Can you tell me some more?" or "How do you do that?" you know you have a winner!

Ideally, your elevator speech should be no more than two or three sentences at the beginning. Remember, the goal is not to say as much as you can in a few seconds, but to start a conversation and generate some interest in what you do. And the sooner you can get the other person responding, the better. The focus should be on your audience. Be a good observer and listener.

In a Nutshell...

1) Once you start asking the right questions, your elevator speech can just jump right out at you!

2) Create shorter versions for quick, ten-second introductions. Your elevator speech is a living statement that can be adjusted to fit each circumstance.

3) Watch how people respond to what you are saying. If they don't ask you more about it, your elevator speech needs more work!

4) Keep it to no more than two or three sentences.

Eighth Floor

Elevator Speeches and
Your Personal Branding

We have explored how elevator speeches help entrepreneurs and businesses stand out from the competition. Now, we'll look at how your elevator speech contributes to your personal brand and can be a critical component in landing that next job or leadership opportunity. Job seekers and people in transition can benefit from a well-crafted statement that articulates your significant qualities or your value in the workplace or to the community. Consider it a key asset in your "personal branding."

The concept of personal branding first hit the national business scene in 1997 when Tom Peters wrote an article titled "The Brand Called You" for *Fast Company* magazine. Many more books and articles have expanded on the idea that, like major corporations, individuals have a brand, an image or impression we make, that sets us apart from the rest of the field.

When you think of national companies like Starbucks, Nike, Apple, WalMart, McDonald's, there's an immediate recognition of the company's personality, its style, and the experience the company wants you to have when you visit its stores. These companies have spent time and a whole lot of money building a recognizable brand.

Whether you realize it or not, you are creating a personal brand. Key elements include your background, your education, the sum of your life experiences, the language you use, your tone of voice, your posture and presence, and whether or not you play well with others.

It's more than your reputation. Your personal brand is a combination of how we see ourselves and how others see us. For example, you may be known as a creative problem-solver, or people may say you're a brilliant closer, or you deliver on your promises. When your actions match what people perceive about you, then you are living your personal brand. In addition, you create an attitude of authentic self-confidence and attract others to you.

While you are out in the business marketplace connecting for the purpose of finding a job or making a career transition, you must know your personal brand and communicate it effectively. Your elevator speech is a quick and easy tool that introduces your personal brand to others. When you can talk about yourself, your interests, and your capabilities in an engaging and memorable way, you are building your personal brand.

When you are interviewing for a job, whether meeting in person, discussing on the phone, interacting on the Web, or appearing on a video, you must demonstrate to a potential employer that you are the best choice. You must understand her problems and quickly articulate how your skills and abilities solve those problems. Even if you are starting out and have little or no employment experience, you can do this effectively.

Remember you need to adapt to different audiences. I recommend that you have at least two versions of your elevator speech, one for casual conversations and another for business settings. In either situation, pay attention to how others react to it and keep experimenting, making small adjustments to it until you get exactly the response you desire.

Let's revisit the foundational questions of the elevator speech questionnaire in "How to Use This Book" in the context of a job search, whether you are entering the job market for the first time or charting a new career path as a seasoned veteran.

It always begins with your audience. Who are they and what do they care about? (See Questions #1 and #2 from the questionnaire.)

When your audience is a prospective employer, you want to learn as much as you can about the company, its culture, and its place in the lifespan of the business. You also want to find out as much as possible about what is going on inside the organization.

Look beyond the company Website. Do a Web search of the company and see what others are saying and research recent news reports. See if you can connect with someone who works there or has firsthand knowledge about the company. With all of the social networking capabilities available today, it is much easier to find someone who can give you an accurate snapshot of the organization.

Gather as much information as you can about the history of the company, its position in the industry, and the current challenges it may be facing. Until you know that information, you cannot accurately gauge whether employment with the firm makes a good match for your skills and interests.

Question #3 can be translated into "Why should they hire you?" How can you benefit this company? What skill, talent, or quality makes you a great hire? Even if this is your first job or you are transitioning to a new industry, you can highlight specific areas that are comparable to what this employer needs.

In the context of a job search or career transition, Questions #4, 5, 7, 8, 9, and 10 can sound very similar. Entrepreneurs and businesses often have different answers for each one as their business grows and expands. When you are starting out in the business world or changing industries, you may not see much differentiation.

For the purpose of building a personal brand, these questions lead you to the various stories you will tell about yourself, your background, and your qualifications. You can encapsulate the ideas behind this series of questions and develop those stories in another way to succinctly define your personal brand and ensure your contacts will remember you.

Years ago when I was laid off in the television industry, I learned a very valuable technique from the unemployment resources offered by the state of California that I still use and recommend today. It is a quick, easy-to-remember formula that helps you develop clear, concise, and relevant stories or anecdotes that you can use to illustrate your value in a job interview, or in any conversation, for that matter.

The technique is called PAR. I've heard of other variations that involve more letters, but I like this one because it's short and easy to remember. *P* stands for Problem. *A* stands for Action. And *R* stands for Results.

This formula helps you tell a relevant story in three sentences or less. PAR has many useful applications, but it is particularly helpful when you are building your personal brand and telling stories about your past accomplishments. It especially helps promote yourself if you have a tendency to be modest or you resist "tooting your own horn."

When talking about your skills and abilities, start with the problem, the negative, and move to your solution, the positive. What issue or problem did you address? What action did you or your team take? And what results did you bring about?

You can use examples from your personal life, your volunteer activities, student projects, or previous employment. You can even use this storytelling technique for hypothetical situations, explaining how you would handle a certain problem: "If this situation occurred, here's one thing I would do about it, and these are the results I would be expecting."

Develop a PAR for each of your key selling points or accomplishments that you want to communicate to potential employers or people who may be in a position to refer you to someone else. Create PARs from all parts of your life and write them down. It boosts your confidence to see your contributions in writing.

If you are new to the workforce, you can create PARs from your student projects or volunteer activities. Instead of focusing on your lack of experience, look at your talent in a broader perspective. Employers are hiring potential, what they believe you will do once on the job, not necessarily what you did do. So they often care more about how you think and how you would work through problems specific to their company or industry.

If you are transitioning to a new career, make PARs relevant to the new industry. Employers value diverse backgrounds. And the stigma of changing industries is diminishing as the whole economy continues to shift and transform. The key is relevance. Can this employer use what you have to offer?

That leaves Question #6. And for this context, I'm changing it to "What spins your jets about the potential of this position or this work?" As mentioned in Chapter Five, your passion is the "secret sauce."

Passion stands out in a sea of mediocrity. When you express it, you engage those around you and attract others to you. People want to hear what you have to say. When you can articulate what would turn you on about a new career opportunity, in an authentic way, you become memorable. It may be the deciding, intangible factor that has a prospective employer choose you. And it will certainly improve your chances of building a strong referral network of supporters who will mention you to others when they hear of opportunities.

Spend a little time and explore what spins your jets!

The Web and social media sites have changed the job search and career transition arena significantly from the old standard. The Web has become an important tool in creating your personal brand.

One caveat ... be careful what you say about yourself or post online. Also monitor what others may be saying or posting about you. Employers now comb sites like Facebook, MySpace, YouTube, etc. to see what applicants are doing in cyberspace. And whatever shows up on a site lives forever online. Protect your personal brand!

In a Nutshell ...

1) Job seekers and people in transition need a great elevator speech.

2) Consider the elevator speech a key component in your personal brand.

3) Live your personal brand.

4) Create PARs to demonstrate your value and key qualities.

5) Protect your personal brand online and in-person.

Ninth Floor

For Presentations and Speeches

The elevator speech process and questionnaire is a product of my public speaking skills and media training and coaching work. I realized that clients' delivery skills improved greatly when they became more confident about what they wanted to say. Their posture was better, the tone of their voice improved, and nervous gestures began to fade away when they became more pleased with the organization and key messages of their presentations.

So I developed a way for clients to create compelling content and shift focus from themselves to their audiences. The next two chapters will explain how to adapt the elevator speech questionnaire and process for speeches, presentations, and media interviews.

The questions you have used to craft your elevator speech will also guide you in developing content for a speech or presentation. As always, you first consider your audience and what is important to them. In this chapter, however, you will ask yourself a series of more specific questions about your audience, then use the answers to add context and depth to your message. When you invest time in researching your audience, you send the signal that you are interested in them and their concerns. Audiences want value from a speaker, and you'll have a difficult time delivering that value unless you know the interests and expectations of your audience.

Once you understand your audience and their concerns, consider the context for your presentation. That means you need to know what is going on in their industry, in their company or organization, in their community, etc. Communication does not happen in a vacuum. Whether you are speaking to employees, coworkers, or an external audience, you must do your homework and find out about the issues impacting your specific audience. Some important questions to ask are:

- Is the business successful?
- Have there been recent layoffs?
- Is there stiff competition in the industry?
- What is their reputation?
- What is the culture of the organization?
- Has there been anything in the news about the company or industry that would impact the audience?
- What is happening in the community at large?
- What's going on in the world that could be relevant to this audience?

Next, consider what questions, concerns, or objections your audience might have about your topic or message. If you can anticipate where an audience might be resistant or even hostile to what you have to say, you can do a great deal to diffuse the situation. One effective way to do this is to respectfully outline the various points of view on all sides of an issue. By taking the initiative and addressing possible problems upfront, you can reduce the tension considerably. This approach keeps the conversation open and gives people room to express their feelings or beliefs. What's important here is that you treat your audience with respect at all times. You don't want to make assumptions or sound as though it's "your way or the highway." As the speaker, you must be considerate of your audience at all times.

In addition to doing audience research, asking yourself the following questions will help round out your preparations and give depth to your message.

- What is your purpose? Or, what are you trying to accomplish with this speech or presentation?
- What would be a successful outcome?

It is the successful blending of your purpose with interests of your audience that creates resonance with your audience.

Work backwards—meaning look at the end result at the beginning—which gives you direction and will likely provide you with powerful ideas to use for your opening and closing remarks in the speech or presentation. People more often respond favorably to a speech when they know where a speaker is taking them. Your purpose may be to inspire, to educate, to persuade, to move your audience to take action, to get a decision. It's not always necessary that you state your purpose openly. But it is important for you as the speaker to have a clear purpose that helps you develop and organize your content.

Next, narrow your focus. The biggest mistake speakers and presenters make is to unload all the information they have on an audience. The old saying "less is more" is particularly relevant to speeches and presentations. People will not remember everything you say. But they will remember whether or not they liked you, whether your information was useful, and whether your delivery seemed credible. If they are sufficiently engaged when you speak, they will pursue your ideas in the future. They may even seek you out for more information.

Keep it simple. What are the two or three key points that you want to communicate? If you are stuck trying to figure out what your main points should be, Dr. Julie Miller, author of *Business Writing That Counts*, suggests using an effective tool called "idea mapping." Let's walk through it.

On a blank sheet of paper—it can be letter-size or a flip chart—draw a circle in the middle of the page. In that circle write the speech, presentation, meeting, or whatever communication situation you are organizing. Like creating spokes on a wheel, start drawing straight lines out from the edge of that circle. As you think of ideas for the presentation, write the idea on one of the lines emanating from the circle. You will find ideas will come to you as you do this. Don't edit at this point; just let it flow. Some of the ideas you have may be offshoots of the bigger ideas. Write those on smaller lines connecting to those ideas.

For example, let's say you are making an announcement about an upcoming conference and you want to recruit volunteers to help. Using the idea mapping strategy, you would draw a circle on a blank piece of paper and inside the circle you would write the word "Conference Announcement."

Next you would draw several lines radiating out from the circle. On those lines you would write the big ideas about the conference, such as "Goals," "Benefits to Volunteers," "Target Audiences," "Logistics," "Tasks. " Under "Goals " you might draw more lines and fill them in with topics like "fundraising," "building community," "raising visibility," Under "Benefits to Volunteers," you can add lines for "build skills," "meet great people," "help a worthy cause." Add whatever ideas apply to the situation. Under "Logistics" you might draw more lines and fill them in with topics like "location," "speakers," "A/V needs." As you think of what is needed for an effective announcement, write it down on a line and soon you will have your thoughts and ideas all in one place to organize your presentation.

There's no right or wrong way to do an idea map. It's all based on what makes sense to you. As you get all of the ideas out of your

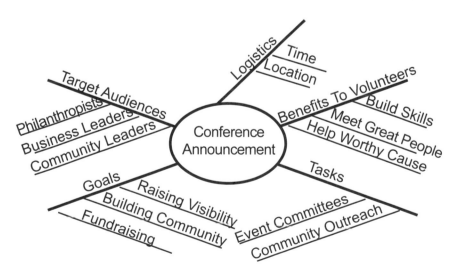

head and onto the paper, you will see common themes and related thoughts beginning to take shape. It's a very powerful way of brainstorming with yourself. If you plan enough in advance, you can do your idea mapping over a period of time. This gives you more freedom to look for and consider as many ideas as possible.

Whether you use a traditional outline or idea mapping to organize your presentation, choose two or three major ideas you want to communicate to your audience. Stick to those ideas and resist the temptation to clutter up your message with everything you want to say. Audiences are willing to listen as long as the information is useful, relevant, or interesting to *them*, not *you*.

One last question to consider—and another way to access your major purpose or objective—is "What do you want people to remember?" As you wrap up your presentation or meeting, think about what thoughts or feelings you want your audience to take away with them. When you have a specific result in mind, that becomes a directional signal for your content. Your intended result will also help you prepare a conclusion that drives home your main points. It's a lot easier to gauge your success when you know where you are going. Whenever possible, get feedback from the meeting participants to see whether or not you hit the mark with your purpose and content.

By now you've probably detected a pattern throughout the book. It's all about the audience. If you can shift your focus from "How am I doing?" to "How are they doing?" you are way ahead of the game. Give them something valuable or useful and they will forgive whatever minor flaws you may have in your delivery technique.

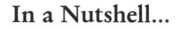

In a Nutshell...

1) The elevator speech process can be adapted and used for speeches, presentations, and media interviews. (Media interview preparation is covered in Chapter Ten.)

2) After you identify your audience and their concerns, consider the context for the presentation by asking questions like these:

   a) Is the business successful?

   b) Have there been recent layoffs?

   c) Is there stiff competition in the industry?

   d) What is their reputation?

   e) What is the culture of the organization?

   f) Has there been anything in the news that would impact the audience?

   g) What is happening in the community at large?

   h) What is going on in the world that could be relevant to this audience?

3) What questions, concerns, or objections might your audience have about your topic or message?

4) What is your purpose for the presentation? What would be a successful outcome?

5) When you identify your optimum results, it will be easier to build a speech or presentation that heads in that direction.

6) "Idea mapping" is a useful tool to generate ideas for speeches and presentations.

7) One final question to answer: What do you want people to remember about your speech or presentation?

Tenth Floor

Helpful Hints for Speaking to the Media

Effective media communications is a huge topic and one that deserves a book of its own. The elevator speech process is an outgrowth of my coaching clients and preparing them for media interviews. If you can narrow your focus and target your message, you can use this tool for communicating with any audience—an individual, a group, or a journalist. The big difference in dealing with media is that you don't have the luxury of time that you do with conversations or presentations. You have to get to the "meat of the matter" immediately. The purpose of this chapter is to explain how the elevator speech process will give you a head start on your preparation for media interviews.

For over twelve years I worked in live television, preparing guests for talk show and news show interviews. I began my production career on an hour-long talk show where we had thirty-five to forty minutes of on-air time for guests to discuss whatever topic had been chosen for the day. That would be considered a huge amount of media time today. The guests and the hosts had not only to engage the audience but also to keep them tuned in to the show. To succeed at this, we emphasized getting to the point as soon as possible. The challenge was to keep the audience from changing channels!

43

Five years of my broadcasting career was spent on a morning news show, where the segments were usually only three to four minutes long. It became critical to have guests who could condense complex ideas and information into much shorter time frames. Today, people have even less time to get to their message. The concept of the "sound bite"—snippets edited into a story—rules. It's really more like "sound bits!"

The elevator speech model will help you identify your key message. When working with media, your target audience will include the viewers or readers of the media outlet of the reporter. So your message may shift a bit depending on the reporter.

The audience for the *Wall Street Journal* is different than the people who read *People* magazine. There are lots of people who read both, but the focus of each publication is different. So you would tailor your message to fit the different interests and expectations of each audience.

If you plan to do a lot of media interviews, it pays to become a student of the various media. Start thinking like a reporter. How does a story begin? Where is the emphasis and focus? Notice the ways in which various media approach the story. Television reporting is different from radio because it requires a visual component. Radio relies on sound for impact. Both differ markedly from print media.

Although similar to print, media on the Web differ from the others in the instantaneous speed with which information moves, the two-way conversation this form allows, and the universality of its readership. Communication via the Web has changed the game completely and contributed significantly to the tremendous turmoil mainstream media like print, broadcast, and cable are experiencing. The old advertising revenue model is disappearing rapidly. Dead or dying traditional newspapers and magazines litter the roadway. And broadcast media is competing with cable and the Web for an audience that is becoming increasingly fragmented.

The good news is that it has become easier to reach your desired audience through bloggers, tweeters, and social networking sites. Now, you just have to understand that your audience will respond back to you, sometimes in ways you don't expect.

Audiences today are looking for value, information that is useful to them. They are very skeptical of old style marketing pitches. They evaluate what businesses offer and also look to their peers online to assess whether or not they will do business with you. If they find something wrong or deficient in what you are doing, they will not hesitate to let you, as well as the rest of the planet, know!

Many of the basics of approaching media on the Web are the same as with traditional outlets. You must have a good story to tell, it needs to be relevant to your intended audience, and they must feel you are operating with integrity.

The effort you put into crafting your elevator speech will help you sharpen your pitch to audiences online and vice versa. Using Twitter offers a great opportunity for you to hone your verbal message while creating an effective summary of yourself on the Web. Take up the challenge to write a clear, concise, and memorable statement in which people find value in 140 characters or less!

And if you post your own video online, please practice first. Amateur video is more accepted today. However, if you are representing your business, consider how your prospective customers will perceive the quality of your online presence.

If you choose any media, new or traditional, to reach your audience, learn how each media outlet operates, what each one looks for in stories and interviews, and how to communicate effectively through that medium.

And make sure you get media training before you talk to any journalist or reporter. A good interview can go a long way to launch you, your product, or your business. A bad interview never dies!

In a Nutshell...

1) For media interviews, you have to get to the meat of the matter quickly. The elevator speech process helps you focus and condense your message.

2) Study media and how they work. Start thinking like a reporter.

3) Prepare for a two-way conversation with your audience when engaging through media on the Web and its social networking sites.

4) Get media training before you ever give an interview.

Eleventh Floor

Just When You Thought You Had It Down

It's time to look at your elevator speech anew! Your elevator speech is a living breathing communications tool. You gauge its effectiveness by the responses you get from people.

When you have something you feel is good—test it. Go to networking events. Try it out and see how people react. Notice the looks on their faces. Do they "get it" or do they look confused? Do they smile and change the subject or do they ask you more about it? Your elevator speech is a conversation starter, not a monologue.

It should also be something that resonates with you. How do you feel when you say it? If it's not authentic or it doesn't sound right coming out of your mouth, then keep working on it. Ask people what would make sense to them or even what would be of interest to them. Don't be afraid to try something new.

Remember, the purpose of an elevator speech is to start a conversation. And people will respond favorably if what you say is interesting and they feel you are being authentic. Be clear and concise and stay focused on your audience. Enjoy the process!

In a Nutshell...

1) Your elevator speech is a living breathing communications tool.

2) Test it and see what responses you get when you use it.

3) Make sure your elevator speech resonates with you first and then speak from your heart. It works every time!

About Lorraine Howell

Lorraine Howell started Media Skills Training in 1998 after twelve years as a television news and talk show producer in the San Francisco Bay Area. She coaches professionals and top executives to speak more effectively in speeches, presentations, and media interviews. In October 2009, she returned for the third year to coach the five finalists in the Forbes.com national Boost Your Business Contest in New York City.

Her book, *Give Your Elevator Speech a Lift!* (Book Publishers Network, 2010, Second Edition), is a step-by-step guide through her proven process for creating a winning elevator speech. Lorraine's method helps eliminate the verbal clutter when answering the question, "What do you do?"

As the Senior Segment Producer on the top-rated news show, *Mornings on 2* at KTVU, the Fox affiliate in Oakland, she specialized in booking exclusive, live interviews with top names in the news, public figures, and celebrities. She produced live broadcasts from the White House and from the Capitol in Washington, D.C., the 1996 Republican and Democratic National Conventions, and "Camp O.J." during the Simpson murder trial in Los Angeles.

At KPIX, the CBS affiliate, she produced live, hour-long programs, featuring breaking news stories, controversial issues and emerging trends, and a long list of celebrities on the number one morning talk show, *People Are Talking*.

Lorraine speaks on media relations and presentation skills at conferences and seminars. Her clients include Starbucks Coffee Company, Microsoft, Group Health Cooperative, Seattle Children's Hospital, Fred Hutchinson Cancer Research Center, University of Washington, ZymoGenetics, Kibble & Prentice, U.S. Small Business Administration, and Edelman Public Relations Worldwide.

She is a Cum Laude graduate from the University of Washington, Phi Beta Kappa. Lorraine is also a member of Women in Communications, Women Business Owners, Public Relations Society of America, and the National Speakers Association.

Lorraine received the national AWC Headliner Award for 2009 from the Association for Women in Communications. In 2008, NSA Northwest named her Chapter Member of the Year.